2015 Viva-eBooks All rights reserved. No part of this book may be reproduced or transferred in any form or by any means, g
hotocopying, scanning, recording, taping or by any other information storage retrieval system with the express written permis
sed are used without any consent and the publication of the trademark is without permission or backing by the trademark ow
ook are for clarifying purposes only and are the property of their respective owners and not affiliated with this document. Viva
r vendor mentioned in this book. The fact that an individual, organisation or website is referred to in this work as a citation an
oes not mean that the author or publisher endorses the information the individual, organisation or website may provide or rec

his book is sold on the understanding that the publisher and author are not engaged in providing medical, legal or other profes
rovided within is for your general knowledge only. The information, advice and strategies contained herein may not suitable for every situation. If you require professional
r medical advice or treatment for a specific condition, the services of a competent, qualified professional person should be sought promptly.

his book is designed to provide general information in regard to the subject matter. While reasonable attempts have been made to verify the accuracy of the information
rovided, neither the author nor the publisher assumes any responsibility for errors, omissions, interpretations or usage of the subject matters within.

Warning on Allergic reactions –

ome recipes included in this book use nuts or nut oils. These specific recipes should be avoided by:
- anyone with a known nut allergy
- anyone who may be vulnerable to nut allergies such as pregnant and nursing mothers, invalids, the elderly, babies and children

ome recipes included in this book use gluten-free oats. However, these specific recipes should be avoided by:
- anyone with a known avenin allergy
- Some recipes used processed ingredients – always check the ingredients list of any processed food to ensure that it is gluten-free as ingredients can vary by manufacturer.

Warning on Eggs – The US Department of Health's advice is that eggs should not be consumed raw. Some recipes included in this book are made with raw or ghtly cooked eggs. These specific recipes should be avoided by:
- anyone who may be vulnerable such as pregnant and nursing mothers, invalids, the elderly, babies and children.

Warning on Blending Hot Foods and Liquids - Remove from the heat and allow to cool for at least 5 minutes. Carefully transfer to a blender or food processor, nsuring that it is no more than half full. If using a blender, release one corner of the lid, which helps prevent heat explosions. Place a towel over the top of the machine, pulse a few times before processing according to the recipe directions.

blog MillyWhiteCooks.com

f facebook.com/MillyWhiteCooks

instagram.com/MillyWhiteCooks

pinterest.com/MillyWhiteCooks

g+ plus.google.com/+MillywhitecooksBooks/posts

twitter.com/MillyWhiteCooks

Contents

Introduction

Why Cook Gluten-Free?

There are a number of reasons why you may want to cook Gluten-Free. These can range from having a medically-diagnosed autoimmune disease through to having a gluten sensitivity or, perhaps making a personal, lifestyle choice.

Celiac/Coeliac Disease or Dermatitis Herpetiformis

If you or a family member has been diagnosed with Celiac Disease (as it is called in the US) or Coeliac Disease (as it is called in the UK) or Dermatitis Herpetiformis, you will already know that these are life-long, gluten-triggered autoimmune diseases. The charity, Coeliac UK, estimates that Celiac/Coeliac Disease affects 1 in 100 people, although only 1 in 4 sufferers have had the condition diagnosed, and that 1 in 10,000 suffers from Dermatitis Herpetiformis. In America, over 3m people have been diagnosed with Celiac Disease. These are life-long conditions, caused by a reaction to the gluten, which is a protein found in wheat, barley and rye. Anyone who is diagnosed with either of these conditions will need to follow a gluten-free diet for the rest of their lives. Celiac/Coeliac Disease does run in families, which unfortunately means that if an immediate blood relative (mother, father, brother, sister) suffers from the disease, then the chances of also having it yourself increase tenfold to 1 in 10. This disease can develop at any age, even in someone who has previously been able to eat gluten without an issue.
Celiac/Coeliac Disease and Dermatitis Herpetiformis are both autoimmune diseases whereby either gluten causes the lining of the gut to be damaged (Celiac/Coeliac Disease) or causes a rash with red, raised patches and/or blisters, most commonly found on knees, elbows, shoulders, bottom and face (Dermatitis Herpetiformis).

Gluten Sensitivity

In addition to the two autoimmune diseases described above, there is growing evidence of non-coeliac gluten sensitivity. This is when someone experiences symptoms similar to Celiac/Coeliac Disease, but there are no associated antibodies and no damage to the lining of the gut. Currently this is much harder to diagnose. However, it is established medical advice that anyone experiencing these symptoms seeks a proper medical diagnosis and is tested for Celiac/Coeliac Disease, <u>before</u> eliminating gluten from their diet.

Choosing to Eat Gluten-Free

Surveys have shown that up to 1 in 3 adults are interested in following a Gluten-Free diet and that interest is growing. In fact, one survey found that 3 out of 4 people who follow a Gluten-Free Diet do so for reasons other than a diagnosed medical condition. Lots of people believe that a Gluten-Free Diet promotes general digestive health and that it reduces toxins in the body.

What About Oats?

Oats do not contain gluten but they do contain the protein avenin, which is similar to gluten. Fortunately, research has shown that it is safe for <u>most</u> people with Celiac/Coeliac Disease to eat avenin. However, there are a very small number of people with Celiac/Coeliac Disease who may still be sensitive to gluten-free, oat products. So, the decision on whether or not to include oats in your diet is something that you do need to discuss with your qualified medical advisers if you suffer from Coeliac Disease. If you can tolerate oats, then they can make a great contribution to a healthy, balanced diet. Oats are an excellent, low-fat source of soluble fibre, which helps to keep a healthy gut. They contain beta glucan which can help lower harmful high cholesterol. As oats are high in soluble fibre, they are slower to digest and can help to keep blood sugars stable. They are a rich, natural source of several essential minerals and vitamins including manganese, zinc and vitamin B1.

However, importantly, if you are able to include oats in your diet, they must be sourced from a certified gluten-free source which ensures that they have not been cross-contaminated with gluten during the manufacturing process.

WHY A GLUTEN-FREE BREAKFAST RECIPE COOKBOOK?

If you're reading this book, it's fair to assume that either you or someone you cook for needs to follow a gluten-free diet. Perhaps you love food and especially love a good breakfast, but feel really limited in your gluten-free choices for breakfast? It can be quite tricky ensuring that meals are gluten-free, and this is especially true at breakfast time. The atypical, modern "Western-diet" breakfast is heavily centered on gluten-rich products, such as breads and wheat-based breakfast cereals. This in itself can be a big enough worry, but on top of that, it can also be ridiculously expensive!

With the rise in awareness of gluten-triggered autoimmune diseases such as Coeliac Disease or Dermatitis Herpetiformis, more and more shops are offering gluten-free alternatives to classic breakfast staples – but, unfortunately, these come at quite a significant price premium. For example, in my research I found the following:

- that a Gluten-Free Seeded Loaf cost 100%-140% more than the "standard" Seeded Loaf
- that Gluten-Free Fruit & Nut Muesli cost 100% more per portion than the "standard" Fruit & Nut Muesli
- that Gluten-Free Granola cost over 100% more per portion than the "standard" Granola.

Although in the UK, gluten-free staple foods (such as bread, breakfast cereals, pasta and pizza bases) are available on prescription for anyone diagnosed with Coeliac disease or Dermatitis Herpetiformis, it remains the case that there is also much less variety and choice in the gluten-free aisle. For example, in my research, I noted that there were over 40 different varieties of "standard" Granola, but just 4 varieties of Gluten-Free Granola. There was definitely a lack of excitement and inventiveness in the flavours and varieties of gluten-free prepared foods on offer in the stores.

When questioned, taste and/or expense are the most often cited reasons why people do not buy a gluten-free product. The good news, though, is that it doesn't have to be that way. It's my belief that Gluten-Free Breakfasts can be:

- Exciting
- Tasty
- Inventive
- Nutritious
- Natural
- Healthy
- Fun

My aim with this book is to provide you with a wide variety of popular, interesting and tasty breakfast meals, all tailored to your needs for a gluten-free diet. However, don't be concerned that you are going to be a slave to the kitchen! My recipes are easy to follow, simple to make and quite a few are multiple servings that can be made ahead of time and stored. What's more, they are all so delicious and nutritious; you can serve them to the whole family, even those who would normally eat gluten, avoiding the need for multiple versions at the breakfast table.

To satisfy cravings for comforting but gluten-containing old-time favourites, I've included recipes that are a reworking of popular classics, such as Fruit & Nut Muesli. You can enjoy all the flavours, textures and tastes of those familiar dishes. But once you've scratched that particular itch, perhaps you'll try something different such as my Spiced Pumpkin, Apple & Walnut Granola as well?

How To Use This Cookbook

Which Wheat-Free Flour?

Most of the recipes in this book that call for flour use a ready-blended plain/all-purpose gluten-free flour mix, such as Bob's Red Mill (US) or Doves Farm (UK). There are two main reasons for this. Firstly, these ready-blended mixes are now very widely available in almost all main supermarkets, meaning that my recipes are easy to use wherever you live or shop (although I have also provided some online stores that carry these ranges in the final section of this book, Resources – Gluten-Free Ingredients). Secondly, using just one all-purpose blend is also friendlier on the wallet, especially when you are starting out on cooking gluten-free. As you continue on your gluten-free journey, you can expand your range of gluten-free flours and start to experiment with them. If you are already a seasoned gluten-free cook, then you may have your own gluten-free blend, in which case, please do use this in place of the proprietary brands.

Other Dietary Considerations

Whilst this book is primarily aimed at gluten-free cooking, I appreciate that you may also be concerned about other dietary needs too. Obviously all the recipes in this book are Gluten-Free and Wheat-Free, meaning no gluten-containing cereals including wheat, rye, barley, spelt, wheat germ, nor any processed ingredient containing these. However, if you have additional dietary requirements or concerns, I have also categorized every recipe into a number of "Free-From" concerns and these are indicated by the following symbols:

Symbols GF DF NF OF V Ve YF

GF Gluten-Free and Wheat-Free, meaning no gluten-containing cereals including wheat, rye, barley, spelt, wheat germ, nor any processed ingredient containing these.

DF Dairy Free meaning no milk, cheese, cream, yogurt, butter nor any other ingredient derived from the milk of cows, goats, ewes or buffalos (or any other milk-producing mammal).

NF Nut Free meaning no peanuts and no tree nuts including almond, brazil nut, cashew, chestnut, coconut, hazelnut, macadamia nut, pecan, pine nut (pignoli), pistachio or walnut nor any processed ingredient containing these. Nutmeg is considered to be a seed rather than a nut, so the ingredients nutmeg and/or mace are classified as nut-free in this book.

OF Oat Free meaning no oats, oat bran nor any processed ingredient containing these.

V Vegetarian meaning no meat, poultry, game, fish or shellfish, nor any by-product from processing such ingredients. However, Vegetarian recipes may include honey, eggs and dairy.

Ve Vegan meaning no meat, poultry, game, fish, shellfish, dairy, honey, eggs nor by-product from processing such ingredients.

YF Yeast Free meaning no yeast nor any processed ingredient containing yeast.

Also, if a recipe does include one or two ingredients that preclude it from being "free-from", where possible, I will include alternative options showing how the recipe can be adapted, for example, non-dairy margarine for butter. Old hands at recipe adapting will already be very familiar with this, so apologies in advance for some fairly obvious substitutions. However, my cook books are bought by a wide variety of readers, but I've included this advice especially if you are either new to cooking for these needs or if you do not regularly cook for these dietary needs and are not used to making such recipe substitutions.

Finally, a note for vegetarians, where a recipe includes cheese but is indicated with the V symbol, it assumes that the cook will use vegetarian cheese if that is required.

Metric vs American Measurements

All recipes are provided in both Metric and American measurements. In order to provide meaningful equivalents, there may be slight "rounding" differences between the two systems, but these do not make a material difference to the overall calorie count. Egg sizes differ between the UK and the US. Most of the recipes in this book are based on UK Large Eggs which is equivalent to American Extra Large Eggs, but the recipe will always advise on the correct egg size.

Both European English and American English names have been given for ingredients where they differ in common usage, for example, Fresh Coriander or Fresh Cilantro.

Standard level spoon measurements are used in all recipes
- 1 tsp = 5ml
- 1 tbsp = 15ml
- A pinch = $\frac{1}{8}$ tsp

Cooking for 1 or 2?

This cookbook provides a variety of recipes whether you are cooking for one, two or more. In addition on recipes serving 4 or more portions, wherever appropriate, recommendations are made for how to freeze and/or store the additional portions for future consumption.

TOP TIPS FOR SAFELY COOKING GLUTEN-FREE

Avoid Cross-Contamination

When you first start cooking gluten-free or if you don't keep an entirely gluten-free kitchen (perhaps as other members of the family do eat gluten), it's very important to avoid cross-contamination between gluten-free and not gluten-free ingredients and kitchen equipment. This may sound straight–forward but it really does require diligence and attention to detail. So, when cooking gluten-free:

- use separate chopping boards, breadboards, non-stick pans, cast iron cookware or any other kitchen utensil/tool that is porous or can be scratched or has "joins" (for example, wood handled silicone spatula, wood rolling pin, wood mixing spoons, metal sieve)
- wash all surfaces thoroughly
- thoroughly clean all cooking utensils and equipment prior to use and then keep them separate during food preparation and cooking
- keep cooking oils and condiments separate
- ideally have a separate grill and toaster for gluten-free cooking but if space or budget won't allow, then use toaster bags to keep gluten-free items uncontaminated.

Read Labels on Processed Foods

Gluten can lurk in the most unlikely processed foods, so take care to carefully read the ingredients lists and allergy advice on all processed foods. For example, as well as the obvious items of bread, cereals and granola, some brands of the following breakfast staples can contain gluten, either due to ingredients with gluten or because of the risk of cross-contamination due the production process:

- baked beans
- tomato ketchup
- Worcestershire sauce
- brown sauce
- sausages
- oats that are not certified as gluten-free
- instant porridge
- flavoured yogurt

Bountiful, Beautiful Brunches & Breakfasts

I'm sure you are familiar with the saying Breakfast like a King, Lunch like a Prince and Dine like a Pauper. When we wake up in the morning, a satisfying breakfast can help provide a great foundation for a good day ahead. There's evidence that it can help with being more active during the day as well as keeping us feeling satisfied until lunch time. When you think about a great breakfast or brunch, do you imagine:

- crisp and crunchy, quick and easy granola on a busy weekday
- creamy, savory eggs, cooked just the way you like them
- light-as-feather, melt-in-your-mouth pancakes and syrup for a weekend brunch
- comforting, delicious, piping-hot baked beans after a brisk Sunday morning walk?

However, did you think that enjoying these mouth-watering breakfast dishes would become a distant memory when on a gluten-free diet? With the enticing recipes in this cookbook, you can think again, as all of these beloved breakfasts and much more can be enjoyed and savored.

In this cookbook, you'll find quick, easy, healthy breakfast dishes perfect for busy weekday mornings as well as more indulgent, comforting recipes especially for social weekend brunches. There are recipes that you can prepare ahead and even ones that cook overnight.

Cooking Techniques

With the recipes in this book, you'll be able to produce great-tasting, gluten-free breakfasts and you don't need to be an experienced cook to do so. In fact for most recipes, the only kitchen skill you'll need is to be able to do a bit of chopping! However, some recipes do require some additional, but still very easy, techniques, mainly separating eggs and then whisking egg whites. If you are fairly new to cooking meals from scratch, here's a quick introduction to these skills (with apologies to the more seasoned cooks who are already familiar with these):

Separating Eggs

Start with the freshest possible, free range eggs, which makes separating them much easier. Make sure you have clean, freshly washed hands, a completely clean, dry bowl for the egg whites and, if you are separating more than one egg, a ramekin or saucer. Separating each egg, one at a time, use a knife to crack the egg open and let the white from one half drop into the ramekin, keeping the yolk in the other half of he shell. Transfer the egg yolk from one half of the shell to the other, tipping any remaining egg white from the shell into the ramekin. Set aside the egg yolk as directed in the recipe, tip the egg white into the lean bowl, then repeat as required. The reason that you use a ramekin is that it is important that bsolutely no yolk makes its way into the separated egg whites. If you break the yolk whilst separating the ggs, then you will have only spoilt the white in the ramekin, not all you egg whites.

Whisking Egg Whites

Once you have separated your egg whites, use a handheld food mixer or stand mixer fitted with the alloon whisk attachment to whisk the egg whites until they form soft peaks. When folding in whisked gg whites, start by just combining 1 tablespoon of whisked whites into your mixture (this is called lackening) before adding the remainder of the whites. Use a gentle folding action when adding egg vhites so that you don't knock out all the lovely air that you've created.

Further Information on Techniques & Ingredients

Please do also take a look at my author blog, MillyWhiteCooks.com.

As well as details on my full range of cookbooks, you will also find articles and helpful information on:

- Ingredients
- Cooking Techniques
- Equipment
- Health News
- Nutrition Information
- Special Offers

Every month I share a new menu of the month, showcasing recipes from my collection. You can find me on social media too:

 MillyWhiteCooks.com

 facebook.com/MillyWhiteCooks

 pinterest.com/MillyWhiteCooks

 instagram.com/MillyWhiteCooks

 twitter.com/MillyWhiteCooks

 plus.google.com/+MillywhitecooksBooks/posts

Your Bonus Gluten Free & Wheat Free FREE Giveaway

As a special Thank You to my readers, I have available an exclusive & free special bonus. Sign up for my Readers Group Newsletter and receive a FREE copy of the Gluten Free & Wheat Free Vegetarian Snacks Recipe Booklet.

To receive your free PDF copy of this booklet, you just need to visit http://goo.gl/Km3H1K and let me know where to email it to.

Brunch Classics

Cinnamon apple pie pancakes drizzled in maple syrup, home cooked beans baked overnight in the slow cooker, brown sugar and vanilla-scented buttermilk French toast – the delicious aromas of a hearty breakfast brunch fill your home with promise of a special and social feast on a leisurely weekend or holiday morning. This chapter provides blissful gluten-free brunch recipes to suit every taste and there are options for many other dietary requirements including Dairy Free, Oat Free, Nut Free, Vegetarian, Vegan and Yeast Free. So welcome friends and family over for an easy, convivial and, most of all, scrumptious breakfast brunch with the recipes in this chapter.

Slow-Cooked Baked Beans on Toast

Ingredients

- 225g (1 Cup) Dried Haricot or Navy or Cannellini Beans
- 400g (3⅓ Cups) Tinned Chopped Tomatoes
- 1 tbsp Tomato Purée
- 1 Garlic Clove, finely chopped
- 2 tsp Cornflour (Cornstarch)
- 2½ tbsp White Wine Vinegar
- 1 tbsp gluten-free Dijon Mustard
- ½ tsp gluten-free Onion Granules
- ¼ tsp Cayenne Pepper
- ¼ tsp Ground Ginger
- 1 tbsp Black Treacle (Molasses)
- Pinch Sea (Kosher) salt
- ½ tsp Ground Black Pepper
- ½ tsp Sea (Kosher) Salt
- 8 Slices Gluten-Free Bread

This recipe cooks overnight in a slow cooker or in a very low oven, you will wake up to the delicious smell of warm beans, then just toast your bread and you are good to go.

Serves: 4 Ready In: 7 hours + soaking time

Directions

Prior to cooking overnight, the beans need to have soaked. To do this, soak them all day in a generous bowl of cold water. Drain, rinse and place in a large saucepan with 2 litres (0.5 gallons) of cold water, bring it to the boil and boil rapidly for 10 minutes.

If you have forgotten to soak the beans all day, don't worry, simply place the beans in a large saucepan with 2 litres (0.5 gallons) of cold water, bring it to the boil and boil rapidly for 10 minutes. Then remove from the heat and set aside for 50 minutes.

Drain the partially cooked beans, reserving 500ml (2 Cups) of the liquid. Put the beans into the slow cooker. In a small jug, dissolve the cornflower in 2 tablespoons of the bean cooled cooking stock or cold water, then add this along with the 500ml (2 Cups) of reserved bean cooking stock or fresh water to the bean mixture. Finely chop or grate the garlic and add this and all the remaining ingredients except the bread slices to the beans. Give everything a really good stir and pop on the lid, set to cook on low for at least 6 hours or overnight.

Alternatively, if you don't have a slow cooker, preheat the oven on low 140C fan, 275F, Gas Mark 1 and cook as directed in a lidded casserole or Dutch oven.

Put on the lid on the slow cooker and if you are cooking in the oven rather than a slow cooker, after 1 hr, reduce the oven temperature to 100C fan, 200F, Gas Mark ¼.

In the morning, check the beans for seasoning and moisture, and add a small pinch of salt and/or a splash of water if required.

Toast the gluten-free bread slices and serve the beans on top of the toasted bread. Add a dash or 2 of Tabasco Sauce if you like a little more spice.

Cooking for 1 or 2? Prepare & Freeze Meal Tip:

Once cooked, divide the Baked Beans into portions for 1 or 2 into microwaveable plastic food trays with lids. Allow to cool and then seal with the tray lids and freeze. To reheat, thoroughly defrost, then either microwave on full for 1-3 mins until hot (dependent on your microwave) or decant into a saucepan and re-warm on the stove top.

HONEYED APRICOT & ALMOND PORRIDGE GF DF V YF

Ingredients

- 80g (1 Cup) Gluten-Free Rolled Oats
- 360ml (1½ Cup) Almond Milk
- 1 Vanilla Bean Pod
- 10g (2 tsp) Natural Caster (Superfine) Sugar
- 6 Ready to Eat Dried Apricots
- 1 tbsp Flaked Almonds
- 2 tsp Golden Linseeds (Flaxseeds)
- 1 tbsp Pure Honey

Directions

Split-open the vanilla bean pod and scrape out the black seeds. Add these to a saucepan along with the oats and milk. Pop the split vanilla seed pod into the pan too, for good measure. Give everything a good stir, and cook over low heat, stirring occasionally, for 8 minutes or until thickened.

Meanwhile, cut the apricots in half. When the porridge is ready, carefully remove the vanilla bean pod and divide the porridge between two warm serving bowls. Spoon over the apricots, drizzle with honey and sprinkle over the flaked almonds and linseeds.

Serves: 2   Ready In: 15 mins

CREAMY GRITS WITH MAPLE SYRUP & PECANS GF DF V Ve YF

Ingredients

- 240ml (1 Cup) Unsweetened Almond Milk
- 240ml (1 Cup) Water
- Pinch Sea (Kosher) Salt (optional)
- 80g (½ Cup) Quick Grits (not instant)
- 1 tbsp Sunflower Spread
- 6 Pecan Halves, chopped
- 1 tbsp Maple Syrup

Directions

In a non-stick milk pan, heat the water and almond milk until it is at a rapid simmer. Stir the liquid briskly with a spatula and pour in the grits, continuing to stir to make sure no lumps form. Reduce heat to medium-low, cover, and simmer for 5 to 7 minutes or until thickened, stirring occasionally.

Remove from heat, stir in the buttery spread and salt, if using. Divide between two bowls, sprinkle over the chopped pecan nuts and swirl over the maple syrup.

Serves: 2   Ready In: 10 mins

Cinnamon Apple Pie Pancakes

GF NF OF V Ve YF

Ingredients

- 1 UK Large (US Extra Large) Free Range Egg, separated
- 50g (¹/₃ Cup) Gluten-Free Plain (All Purpose) Flour Blend
- 10g (2 tsp) Natural Caster (Superfine) Sugar
- ¼ tsp Bicarbonate of Soda (Baking Soda)
- ½ tsp gluten-free Baking Powder
- 100g (¹/₃ Cup + 1 tbsp) Buttermilk
- ¼ tsp Xanthan Gum
- ½ tsp Ground Cinnamon
- 10g (1 tbsp) Raisins
- 30g (2 tbsp) Greek Yogurt
- ½ tsp fresh Orange Zest
- ½ tsp Vanilla Extract
- 1 Medium Apple
- 2 tbsp Maple Syrup
- 1 tsp Olive Oil

Directions

Preheat the oven on low 80C fan, 175F, Gas Mark ¼. Put an oven-proof serving plate into warm.

Sieve together the flour, xanthan gum, baking powder and baking soda into a bowl. Mix in the caster (superfine) sugar and cinnamon. Separate the egg, putting the yolk into a jug and the white into a separate clean bowl. Whisk the egg white until stiff. Combine the egg yolk with the buttermilk, vanilla extract and finely grated orange zest, then pour into the flour/sugar mixture. Whisk until smooth. Grate the apple (skin on) and add to the mixture along with the raisins. Finally, carefully fold in the stiff egg white.

Heat the olive oil in a large frying pan over a medium heat. Drop in spoonfuls of batter, so each pancake is about ¼ of the mixture. Cook for 2-3 minutes, until bubbles start to appear on the top of the pancake, then flip over and cook for another 2 mins until golden. Remove and keep warm. Repeat to make 4 pancakes. Serve two pancakes per person, drizzled with maple syrup and topped with Greek Yogurt.

Cooking for 1? Prepare & Store Meal Tip:

Wait until the 2 uneaten pancakes are cool and wrap individually in kitchen wax paper then store in a sealable airtight container in the fridge for 1-2 days. To serve, warm a non-stick sauté pan over a low-medium heat and warm the pancakes through before serving.

Serves: 2   Ready In: 15 mins

Kedgeree with Dairy-Free Raita

GF **DF** **NF** **OF** **YF**

Ingredients

- 115g (4 zz) Un-Dyed Smoked Haddock
- 85g (½ Cup) Brown Basmati Rice
- 50g ($^1/_3$ Cup) Frozen Peas
- 60g (2 Cup) Baby Spinach Leaves
- 1 UK Large (US Extra Large) Free Range Egg
- 1 tsp Olive Oil
- ½ medium Red Onion
- 1 Garlic Clove
- ½ tsp Ground Coriander
- ½ tsp Ground Turmeric
- 1 tsp Mild Curry Powder
- 2 Cardamom Pods
- 1 dash Tabasco Sauce
- 1 Bay Leaf
- 3 Whole Peppercorns
- ¼ English Cucumber
- 1 tbsp Parsley, chopped
- 1 tbsp Mint, chopped
- 2 tbsp Coriander (Cilantro), chopped
- 80g ($^1/_3$ Cup) Natural Dairy-Free Yogurt

Directions

Preferably, make the raita the night before to allow the flavours to develop. Split the cucumber lengthwise. Scoop out the seeds with a spoon and discard. Pat the halves dry with a piece of kitchen towel, then coarsely grate the cucumber into a sealable container. Finely chop the coriander and mint and stir through the grated cucumber along with the natural yogurt. Seal the container and chill.

Preheat the oven on low 100C fan, 200F, Gas Mark ¼. Put an oven-proof serving platter into warm. Bring the frozen peas out to partially defrost.

Place the haddock, bay leaf and peppercorns into a sauté pan, cover with water, and over medium heat, gently poach for 10 mins until the flesh flakes. Remove the fish to the warm serving dish, cover with aluminium foil and return to the oven to keep warm. Pour the cooking liquid into a jug, retaining the bay leaves but discarding the peppercorns. You will need 180ml (¾ cup) of cooking liquid in total, so top up with boiling water if required.

Next, finely dice the red onion. Wipe out the sauté pan then return to a medium heat and add the olive oil. Gently sauté the onion, for 5 mins until softened. Finely mince the garlic. Crack open the cardamom seed pods with the back of a spoon, then add these whole along with the remaining spices and minced garlic to the onion. Stir well and continue to sauté for a further 3 mins until the mix turns golden. Add the rice to the pan and stir well to combine, so that all the grains are covered in the spicy onion mixture. Add the fish stock and the bay leaves, stir and bring to a simmer, then cover the pan and cook for 20 mins. Without stirring, lift off the pan lid, add the partially frozen peas and the baby spinach leaves and replace the pan lid. Remove the pan from the heat and set aside 5 mins to finish cooking.

Meanwhile, put the egg into a saucepan, cover with water, bring to the boil, then reduce to a simmer for 5 mins. Use a slotted spoon to remove the egg from the boiling water and plunge into cold water. Once cool enough to handle, peel the egg and cut into quarter wedges.

Remove the fish from the oven, peel away the skin and flake the flesh into bite size pieces, taking care to remove any bones. Remove the bay leaves and cardamom pods from the rice, and fluff it up with a fork, mixing in the peas and now wilted spinach. Add the chopped parsley and fish, then gently fork through. Transfer to the warm serving dish and scatter over the egg quarters. Serve with the chilled raita.

Serves: 2   Ready In: 45 mins

Breakfast Corn Fritters

Ingredients

- 90g (¾ Cup) Maize Flour (or Gluten-Free Plain/All Purpose Flour Blend)
- 1 tsp Gluten-Free Baking Powder
- 1 tsp Cornflour/ Cornstarch
- 1 UK Large (US Extra Large) Free Range Egg
- 150ml (½ Cup + 2 tbsp) Buttermilk
- 250g tinned Sweetcorn, rinsed and drained
- 1 tbsp Olive Oil
- ½ tsp Smoked Paprika
- ¼ tsp freshly Ground Black Pepper
- ⅛ tsp Sea (Kosher) Salt

Directions

Preheat the oven on low 80C fan, 175F, Gas Mark ¼. Put an oven-proof serving plate into warm.

In a roomy bowl, sift the flour, baking powder, paprika and cornflour/cornstarch, make a well in the center. Whisk together the egg and buttermilk, then pour onto the well in the dry ingredients. Beat well to combine. Fold in the sweetcorn and season with salt and pepper.

Heat 1 tsp of olive oil in a large non-stick frying pan over a medium heat, then spoon 2 tbsp of the mixture for each fritter into the hot pan. Cook 4 fritters at a time, cooking for 1-2 mins on one side, then flip and cook until golden. Remove onto the warm serving plate and keep warm in oven on until all are ready to serve. Repeat with a further tsp of olive oil and another 4 fritters, then repeat again. Serve hot.

Make this Dairy-Free? – Use Soya or Almond Milk in place of the Buttermilk.

Serves: 4   Ready In: 25 mins

Buttermilk French Toast with Honey Blueberry Compote

Ingredients

- 180ml (¾ Cup) Buttermilk
- 2 Medium (Large) Eggs
- 1 UK Medium (US Large) Free Range Egg White
- 1 tbsp Brown Sugar
- ½ tsp Ground Cinnamon
- Pinch Freshly Grated Nutmeg
- 60ml (4 tbsp) Greek Yogurt
- ½ tsp Vanilla Extract
- 6 Slices Gluten-Free Bread
- 1 tsp Olive Oil
- 140g (1 Cup) Fresh or Frozen Blueberries
- 2 tbsp Honey
- 2 tsp Lemon juice

Directions

Preheat the oven on low 80C fan, 175F, Gas Mark ¼. Put an oven-proof serving plate into warm.

Line a baking sheet with non-stick paper. In a wide, shallow bowl, combine together the buttermilk, eggs, brown sugar, cinnamon, nutmeg, and vanilla extract in a medium bowl. Whisk together until thoroughly combined. Cut the bread slices into half across the diagonal to form triangles. Dip each bread triangle into the eggy mixture for about 10 seconds then flip over for a further 10 seconds until the bread triangles are nicely soaked. Place each eggy triangle on the lined baking sheet until all are finished and chill whilst you make the blueberry compote.

Place 20ml (1 tbsp + 1 tsp) water in a small saucepan along with half of the blueberries, honey and lemon juice . Cook over a medium heat, bring to the boil, then reduce the heat to a gentle simmer and stew the fruits for 10 mins, stirring with a spatula. Add the rest of the blueberries and cook for 3 mins more. Set aside.

Heat a large, non-stick frying pan over medium heat and spritz with 2 sprays of Fry Light Olive Oil Spray. Cook triangles in batches until golden brown on both sides (about 3 mins per side). Keep warm in oven in until all are ready to serve.

Serve 3 French Toast Triangles per person, with a tablespoon of Greek yogurt and the blueberry compote.

Serves: 4   Ready In: **30 mins**

Baked Huevos Ranchero

GF DF NF OF V YF

Ingredients

- 250g (1 Cup) tinned, reduced salt, chopped Tomatoes
- 180g (1½ Cups) Chestnut (Baby Portabella) Mushrooms
- 100g (½ Cup) tinned black beans, rinsed and drained
- 2 Red or Green (Jalapeno) Chillies
- ½ tsp Chilli Powder (ancho or mild chilli powder)
- 1 tsp Natural Caster (Superfine) Sugar
- ½ gluten-free Vegetable Stock Cube
- 40g (2 Cups) Fresh Coriander (Cilantro)
- 4 UK Medium (US Large) Free Range Eggs

- 1 Red Onion
- 1 Red Bell Pepper
- 1 Lime, divided
- 1 Garlic Clove
- 1 tsp Ground Cumin
- ¼ tsp Cayenne Pepper
- 1 tsp Olive Oil
- ½ tsp Freshly Ground Black Pepper
- ¼ tsp Sea (Kosher) Salt, divided

Directions

Dice the onion. Deseed the red pepper and cut into strips. Heat the olive oil in an oven-proof sauté pan or shallow cast-iron casserole (Dutch Oven) over a medium heat. Add the chopped onions and peppers and sauté, stirring, for 3 to 5 minutes. Clean the mushrooms, slice them and add them to the pan. Continue to sauté for a further 5 mins. Meanwhile, remove the leaves from the fresh coriander (cilantro) and set aside. Finely mince the coriander (cilantro) stalks along with the garlic and the chilli peppers. Add these to the pan along with the ground cumin and cayenne pepper and cook for a further minute. Add the tinned tomatoes with their juices, the rinsed and drained black beans, ½ tsp freshly ground black pepper, $\frac{1}{8}$ tsp salt and 1 tsp of natural caster (superfine) sugar. Give everything a good stir. Dissolve the ½ stock cube in 120ml (½ cup of boiling water) and add to the pan. Simmer the stew until thickened, about 15 minutes.

Preheat the oven to 180C fan, 400F, Gas Mark 6.

Chop the retained coriander leaves, set aside 1 tbsp and stir the remainder into the stew along with the juice of ½ lime. Prepare the eggs by breaking each egg into its own cup or ramekin (so that you can work quickly). Make 4 wells in the Ranchero stew, quickly pour an egg into each well and pop into the hot oven or to cook for 12-15 minutes (or a little longer, depending on how you like your eggs).

When the eggs are cooked to your liking, serve on warm plates. Add a dash or two of Tabasco Sauce if you like a little more heat.

Serves: 4   Ready In: 45 mins

Potato Farls with Sautéed Mushrooms

Ingredients

- 3 Medium Potatoes (c 300g/ 10.5oz)
- 240g (2 Cups) Chestnut (Baby Portabella) Mushrooms
- 70g (½ Cup) Gluten-Free Plain (All Purpose) Flour Blend + extra for rolling
- ½ tsp gluten-free Baking Powder (Soda)
- 1 tsp Olive Oil
- 3 tsp Sunflower Spread, divided
- 2 tsp fresh Thyme, chopped
- ¼ tsp Sea (Kosher) Salt, divided
- ½ tsp Freshly Ground Black Pepper, divided

Directions

Peel the potatoes and cut into large chunks. Place into a saucepan with fresh cold water and a pinch of salt. Bring the boil and simmer for 8-10 mins. Meanwhile, clean the mushrooms and cut into half. Warm 2 tsp of sunflower spread in sauté pan over a medium heat, then add the mushrooms and toss in the melted spread. Turn the heat down to low and leave the mushrooms to sauté, using a spatula to occasionally turn them. Add a splash of water if the mushrooms become to dry.

When the potatoes are completely tender, strain them then weigh out 250g (9oz) of cooked potatoes and return to the hot pan. Allow the potatoes to steam-dry for 1 min. Using a hand-mixer or potato masher, thoroughly mash the potatoes and add 1 tsp of sunflower spread. Whisk together the flour blend, baking powder (soda), salt and ground black pepper, then add to the potato mash. Beat together to form a soft dough. Transfer to a lightly floured surface and roll-out or pat-out the dough into a circle about 1cm (¹/₃") deep and 15-20cm (6-8") wide. Cut into 4 equal wedges.

Heat 1 tsp of olive oil in a non-stick frying pan over a medium heat. Cook the farls for 3-5 mins on each side until lightly golden brown and cooked through. Serve the farls onto warm serving plates, and spoon the mushrooms to the side, and sprinkle with chopped fresh thyme.

Serves: 2   Ready In: 25 mins

Breakfast Fruits

Fruity breakfasts are healthy, energising and often quick and easy way to start the day, getting several of your 5-a-day under your belt from the get-go. Fruit breakfasts are also often beautifully portable, so make a great choice if you need breakfast on the go too. Make your fruity breakfast extra satisfying and stay fuller longer by combining with seeds, oats, quinoa or yogurt. And don't think that a fruit breakfast means a cold breakfast, we're kicking off with a warm, delicious and oh-so-satisfying apple and fig breakfast crumble.

Ginger Zinger Fresh Fruit Salad

Ingredients   YF

- ½ Lime
- ½ Orange
- 1 Kiwi Fruit
- 1 Large Mango
- 100g Blueberries
- 1 tbsp Fresh Ginger, grated
- 1 tsp Golden Linseeds (Flaxseeds)

Directions

This can be prepared the evening before and stored overnight in a sealable container, if required.

Peel the fresh ginger root and grate it along with the zest from the lime. Juice the lime and the half orange and mix with the ginger and lime zest.

Peel the kiwi fruit, cut in half and slice. Peel the mango and cut into bite size pieces. In a bowl, mix together all the ingredients. Allow the flavours to develop for 30mins (or overnight), sprinkle with flaxseeds then serve.

Cooking for 1? Prepare & Store Meal Tip:

You can store ½ of this fruit salad in a sealable airtight container and store in the fridge for up to 3 days.

Serves: 2   Ready In: 35 mins

Apple & Fig Breakfast Crumble GF DF V Ve YF

Ingredients

- 50g (¼ Cup) Natural Caster (Superfine) Sugar, divided
- 65g (¾ Cup) Dairy-Free Buttery Sunflower Spread
- 30g (¼ Cup) Gluten-Free Plain (All Purpose) Flour Blend
- 60g (¾ Cup) Gluten-Free Rolled Oats
- 25g ($^1/_3$ Cup) Quinoa Flakes
- 2 tsp Golden Linseeds (Flaxseeds)
- 25g (¼ Cup) Walnut Nut Halves

- 3 Medium Red Apples
- 8 Dried Figs
- 1 tbsp Pumpkin Seeds
- 2 tsp Sunflower Seeds
- 1 tsp Ground Cinnamon
- 4 tbsp Greek Yogurt

Directions

Preheat the oven to 180C fan, 350F, Gas Mark 6.

Peel, quarter, core and slice the apples. Quarter the dried figs. In a bowl, toss the fruit together with half the sugar. Divide the fruit between 4 oven-proof ramekins on a baking sheet. Place in the oven for 10 mins.

Meanwhile, mix together the flour, oats and quinoa flakes. Add the cold sunflower spread and rub in with your fingertips until the mixture resembles fine breadcrumbs. Chop the walnut pieces and add these to the oat mix together with the remaining sugar, seeds and ground cinnamon. Mix until well combined.

Carefully remove the baking sheet from the oven and evenly divide the topping over the fruit in the ramekins. Return to the oven and bake for a further 20-25 mins until golden brown and bubbling. Serve with 1 tbsp Greek Yogurt.

Make this Oat-Free? – Omit the oats and replace with quinoa flakes.

Serves: 4   Ready In: 40 mins

Apricot, Peach & Honey Parfaits

GF **DF** **NF** **V** **YF**

Ingredients

- 4 Ready to Eat Dried Apricots
- 1 Firm Ripe Fresh Peach
- 1 tbsp Honey
- ½ Vanilla Bean Pod
- 1 tbsp Gluten-Free Porridge Oats (optional)

- ½ Lemon
- ½ Cinnamon Stick
- 1 tbsp Sunflower Seeds
- ½ tsp Ground Cinnamon
- 120g (½ Cup) Greek Yogurt

Directions

Make the peach/apricot compote the night before and store overnight in the fridge.

To peel the peach, bring a pan of water to boil and add the peach, blanch for 1 min, then remove with a slotted spoon. When cool enough to handle, slip off the skin, then cut in half and remove the stone. Cut each half into four segments. Cut the dried apricots in half. Place the fruit into a saucepan, along with the zest and juice of the ½ lemon, honey and ½ cinnamon stick. Split the ½ vanilla pod in half length wise, scrape out the seeds and add these and the pod to the fruit. Bring up to the simmer over a low heat, stirring gently. Simmer for 5 mins or until the peach is tender. Leave to cool, then store in a sealable container in the fridge overnight.

Meanwhile, heat a non-stick sauté pan over a medium heat and toast the porridge oats (optional) and sunflower seeds. Keep tossing the oats and seeds, taking care not to burn them. When cooked, remove to a ramekin and stir in the ½ tsp of ground cinnamon. Set aside until the morning.

In the morning, divide half of the fruit compote between 2 serving glasses, followed by half of the Greek yogurt and then repeat. Sprinkle the cinnamon oats/seeds over the top and serve.

Make this Dairy-Free/Vegan? – Simply use a dairy-free alternative to Greek yogurt, and substitute maple syrup for the honey to make it Vegan too.

Serves: 2   Ready In: 15 mins plus chilling time

Fresh Citrus Salad with Quick Fruit Compote

 **GF DF OF V YF**

Ingredients

- 60g ($^1/_3$ Cup) Ready to Eat Dried Prunes
- 60g (½ Cup) Ready to Eat Dried Apricots
- 30g (3 tbsp) Golden Raisins
- 2 Oranges
- 1 Pink Grapefruit
- 2 tbsp Flaked Almonds
- 1 tbsp Sunflower Seeds
- 1 tbsp Honey

Directions

Place the prunes, apricots and raisins in a small saucepan. Zest one of the oranges and add this and the juice from the same orange to the saucepan. Add the honey and give everything a good stir. Warm the fruits over a medium heat until it comes to a gentle simmer, then turn off the heat and leave to soak and plump up.

Use a sharp knife to cut the peel and pith away from the pink grapefruit and remaining orange. Slice both fruits into thin rounds and divide between two breakfast bowls along with any juices. Spoon over the fruit compote, then scatter over the flaked almonds and sunflower seeds.

Make this Vegan? - Substitute maple syrup for the honey to make it Vegan too.

Prepare & Store Meal Tip:

This can be made the night before (up to the stage of scattering with the nuts and seeds) and stored overnight in the fridge in a sealed container.

Serves: 2   Ready In: 15 mins

Roasted Rhubarb with Honey Greek Yogurt

Ingredients

- 125g (1 Cup) fresh Rhubarb
- 1 Clementine
- 1 tbsp Natural (Superfine) Caster Sugar
- 1 tbsp Honey
- 240ml (1 Cup) Greek Yogurt

Directions

Preheat the oven to 180C fan, 350F, Gas Mark 6.

Finely grate the zest from the Clementine and set aside for latter. Cut the rhubarb into 5cm/2" pieces and place into a small roasting dish. Sprinkle over the sugar. Peel the Clementine and slice into thin rounds. Place over the rhubarb. Cover the roasting dish with kitchen foil and bake in the oven for 25mins.

Meanwhile, whisk together the retained Clementine zest, honey and Greek yogurt, Cover with kitchen film and store in the fridge until required.

When the rhubarb is cooked, remove from the oven, take off the foil and set aside to rest for 5 mins. Then divide between 2 dishes and spoon the honey Greek Yogurt to the side.

Make this Vegan? - Substitute maple syrup for the honey to make it Vegan too.

Serves: 2   Ready In: 35 mins

Juices & Smoothies

Tangy or creamy, zingy or smooth, juices and smoothies taste sensational and are a super-quick and easy way to start the day. However, if you buy your juices and smoothies from the store, not only is it often very expensive but you also lose the vitality, freshness and healthiness that comes from a home-made juice or smoothie. The recipes in this section are packed full of wholesome, flavoursome, energising ingredients, brimming with essential vitamins, minerals and enzymes. They will make your day start with a Wow!

Dairy-Free Vegan Maple Cinnamon Smoothie

Ingredients

- 1 Banana
- 180ml (¾ Cup) Unsweetened Almond Milk
- ½ tsp Ground Cinnamon
- pinch Freshly Grated Nutmeg
- ¼ tsp Vanilla Extract
- 1 tsp Maple Syrup

Directions

The evening before, peel the banana and cut into 3 pieces and pop it into your freezer. In the morning, place all the ingredients except the nutmeg into a blender and whizz together until smooth. Pour into a glass, grate a sprinkle of fresh nutmeg over the top and serve.

Serves: 1   Ready In: 2 mins

ZINGY APPLE, CARROT & GINGER JUICE

Ingredients

- 2 Apples
- 2 Oranges

- 2 Carrots
- 2.5cm (1") piece fresh Ginger Root

Directions

Scrape the skin from the ginger root. Peel and segment the orange. Wash the apples and carrots, then cut the apples into quarters and remove the core. Put all the ingredients through a juicing machine, then pour into 2 glasses.

Serves: 2   Ready In: 5 mins

VANILLA PEACH PARFAIT SMOOTHIE

Ingredients

- 120ml (¼ Cup) Milk
- 120g (¼ Cup) Plain Yogurt
- 1 Medium Banana

- 1 Peach
- 1 tsp Vanilla Extract
- 2 tsp Honey

Directions

If you can, the evening before, peel the banana and cut into 3 pieces and pop it into your freezer. In the morning, peel the peach, cut in half and remove the stone. Place all the ingredients into a blender and whizz together until smooth. Pour into a glass and serve.

Make this Dairy-Free/Vegan? – Simply use a dairy-free alternative to the Milk & Yogurt and substitute maple syrup for the honey to make it Vegan too.

Serves: 2   Ready In: 2 mins

Dairy-Free Coconut, Pear & Spinach Smoothie

GF DF NF **OF** V YF

Ingredients

- 240ml (1 Cup) Coconut Milk Drink Alternative
- ½ English Cucumber
- 120g (4 Cups) Baby Spinach
- 2.5cm (1") piece fresh Ginger Root
- 2 ripe, medium Pears
- 1 Lemon
- 4 tsp Ground Flaxseeds
- 4 tsp Honey

Directions

Scrape the skin from the ginger root and finely grate. Wash the pears and cucumber, pat dry. Cut the pear into quarters, remove the core and roughly chop along with the cucumber. Squeeze the juice from the lemon. Put all the ingredients through a blender and whizz together until smooth. Add more coconut milk drink if you would like a thinner-textured smoothie. Pour into 2 glasses and serve.

Serves: 2   Ready In: 2 mins

Dairy-Free Tropical Smoothie

GF DF NF **OF** V YF

Ingredients

- 120g (½ Cup) Plain Coconut Milk Yogurt
- 120ml (½ Cup) Pineapple Juice
- 1 tbsp unsweetened Desiccated Coconut
- 1 Banana
- 1 ripe, medium Mango

Directions

The evening before, peel the banana and cut into 3 pieces and pop it into your freezer. In the morning, place all the ingredients into a blender and whizz together until smooth. Pour into 2 glasses and serve.

Serves: 2   Ready In: 2 mins

Breakfast Salads

Perhaps salad for breakfast just sounds wrong to you, but hopefully these energising recipes will make you change your mind. These are a great choice if your palette enjoys sweet and savoury flavour combinations or if you find fruit salad alone not substantial enough for breakfast, as breakfast salads pack a powerful punch, combining salad vegetables with fruits, healthy fats, proteins and low-GI carbs.

BLT Breakfast Salad

GF DF NF OF YF

Ingredients

- 3-4 Romaine Lettuce Leaves
- 2 Rashers Bacon
- 1 Free Range Egg
- 3 Plum Tomatoes
- 1 tsp Olive Oil
- 2 tsp Balsamic Vinegar
- ¼ tsp Gluten Free Mustard Powder
- 1 stick of Celery Heart
- freshly ground Black Pepper

Directions

Start this recipe by putting the egg onto poach. Fill a saucepan with 5cm/2" of boiling water and place over a low heat. Crack the egg into a ramekin. Put the bacon rashers onto grill.

When the water in the saucepan is at scalding point (that is, there are occasional small bubbles forming but it is not at a full boil), swirl the water rapidly with a spoon to create a vortex and quickly tip in the egg. Leave on the heat for 2 mins, then remove from the heat, cover with the lid and set aside for 8-10 mins (depending on how well cooked you like your egg). Meanwhile, in a clean ramekin, whisk together the mustard powder, oil and vinegar, season with freshly ground black pepper. Use a vegetable peeler to "de-thread" the celery heart stalk – this means running the vegetable peeler over the ribbed side of the celery to remove the stringy bits. It takes less than a minute to do this and makes raw celery so much nicer to eat. Dice the celery, cut the tomatoes in half and shred the lettuce leaves.

Spread the lettuce leaves over a plate and scatter over the tomatoes and celery. Once the bacon is grilled, cut into strips and scatter over the salad too. When the egg is cooked, use a slotted spoon to carefully lift it out of the water. Place the spoon onto a sheet of kitchen towel to absorb any water left on the egg then transfer onto the centre of the salad. Spoon the dressing over the egg and tomatoes, and season the egg with a fresh grinding of black pepper. Serve immediately.

Make this Vegetarian? – Substitute Quorn Rashers for the Bacon.

Serves: 1   Ready In: 15 mins

Honeyed Beetroot, Apple & Walnut Salad Bowls

Ingredients

- 175g (6 oz) ready cooked Beetroot (not pickled or in vinegar)
- 100g (3 cups) fresh Lambs Lettuce (or any small baby leaf lettuce)
- 1 Green Apple
- 8 Walnut Halves
- Pinch Freshly Ground Black Pepper

- 1 Lemon, Divided
- 1 tbsp Honey
- ½ tbsp Walnut Oil
- 80g ($^1/_3$ Cup) Plain Yogurt
- ½ tsp Dried Tarragon
- Pinch Sea (Kosher) Salt

Directions

(You may want to wear rubber kitchen gloves when handling the beetroot!) Over the sink, carefully remove the beetroot from packaging. Rinse, drain and pat dry with kitchen towel. Cut into wedges.

Cut the lemon in half and set aside one half. Juice the remaining lemon half into a bowl and whisk in the honey, walnut oil, dried tarragon and a pinch of salt and pepper to form a vinaigrette. Add the beetroot wedges and toss.

Put the yogurt into a ramekin and finely grate over the zest from the remaining lemon half, then squeeze over the juice and whisk together.

Roughly chop the walnuts. Heat a non-stick sauté pan over a medium heat and add the walnuts. Toast the walnuts for 3-4 mins, keeping a careful eye on them to ensure that they don't burn. Meanwhile, core the apple and slice into segments. Divide the Lambs Lettuce between two bowls and spoon over the dressed beetroot wedges and any juices from the bowl. Scatter over the sliced apples and toasted walnuts. Finally, spoon over the yogurt dressing and serve.

Make this Vegan? – Substitute Maple Syrup for the Honey.

Serves: 2   Ready In: 15 mins

Mango, Blueberry & Avocado Salad Cups

 GF **OF** V YF

Ingredients

- ½ ripe Avocado Pear
- 75g (½ cup) Blueberries
- ½ ripe Mango
- 70g (2 cups) Baby Kale Leaves
- 1 tsp Poppy Seeds
- 2 tsp Honey
- 4 tsp Greek Yogurt
- 4 tsp Orange Juice
- $\frac{1}{8}$ tsp Ground Cinnamon
- $\frac{1}{8}$ tsp Sea (Kosher) Salt
- ¼ tsp freshly ground Black Pepper

Directions

Put the yogurt into a small jug and whisk in the orange juice, honey, cinnamon, salt and pepper. Put the baby kale leaves into a roomy bowl and pour over half the dressing. Toss well, then divide between two large breakfast cups.

Peel the mango and avocado, cut in half across the middle, then thinly slice (so you have neat, bite-size slices of avocado and mango). Divide between the two cups along with the blueberries. Scatter over the poppy seeds and drizzle the salad with the remaining dressing then serve.

Make this Vegan? – Substitute Maple Syrup for the Honey and dairy-free yogurt for the Greek yogurt.

Serves: 2   Ready In: **15 mins**

Toasted Quinoa & Autumn Fruits Breakfast Salad

Ingredients

- 30g (1 Cup) Baby Spinach
- 1 tbsp dry Quinoa
- 1 Plum
- 3-4 Strawberries
- 6-8 Red Grapes
- 1 Clementine
- ½ tbsp Rapeseed Oil
- 1 tsp Maple Syrup
- ¼ tsp gluten-free Dry Mustard Powder
- freshly ground Black Pepper

Directions

Start this recipe by cleaning and toasting the quinoa. This step (and the making of the dressing) can easily be done on the evening before and stored in the fridge overnight, making this a super-quick morning recipe.

Put the quinoa into a small jug or ramekin and cover with cold water. Set aside to soak for 10 mins or so.

Peel the ¾ quarters of the Clementine and remove the exposed fruit, leaving ¼ still in its peel. Squeeze the juice from this remaining quarter into a bowl and whisk in the oil, maple syrup, mustard powder and black pepper. Add the clean spinach leaves to the bowl and toss well.

Stir the soaking quinoa to remove any residue, then drain through a wire sieve and rinse thoroughly. Heat a non-stick sauté pan over a medium heat and tip in the soaked and cleaned quinoa. Spread out into an even layer and let it start to toast, stirring regularly to prevent sticking. It will start to pop (a little may escape from the pan during this popping stage) and then start to turn a lovely nutty brown colour. When the quinoa is evenly toasted, remove from the heat.

Whilst the quinoa is toasting, prepare the fruit, dividing the Clementine into segments, cutting the grapes in half, stoning and slicing the plum and hulling and slicing the strawberries. Once the quinoa has toasted, place the dressed spinach leaves onto a plate and arrange your fruit prettily over the top, then scatter over the toasted quinoa and serve.

Serves: 1   Ready In: 20 mins

Tropical Fruit Breakfast Salad with Warm Granola Sprinkle GF DF V Ve YF

Ingredients

- 75g (½ cup) Papaya
- 80g (½ cup) Pineapple
- 90g (3 cups) Baby Spinach Leaves
- 2 tsp Unsweetened Desiccated Coconut
- 1 tsp Palm Syrup or Maple Syrup
- ¼ tsp freshly ground Black Pepper
- 1 small Banana
- ½ Lime
- 4 tbsp gluten-free Oats
- 2 tbsp Pistachio Nuts
- 2 tsp Coconut Oil

Directions

Preheat the oven to 160C fan, 350F, Gas Mark 6.

In a bowl, finely grate the zest from the lime and then squeeze over the juice. Whisk in the coconut oil. Transfer half of this mixture to an oven-proof ramekin, then add to the ramekin the palm/maple syrup and whisk again. Roughly chop the pistachio nuts and add these to the ramekin along with the oats and desiccated coconut. Stir well to combine, then place into the oven and bake for 10 mins, stirring half way through the cooking time.

Add the spinach leaves to the reserved dressing, season with freshly ground black pepper and toss well.

Peel and slice the banana, papaya and pineapple into bite size pieces. Divide the dressed spinach leaves between two bowls and top with the fruits. When cooked, remove the baked granola from the oven and set aside to cool for 2-3 mins, then sprinkle over the salad and serve.

Make this Oat-Free? – Omit the oats and replace with quinoa flakes.

Serves: 2   Ready In: 15 mins

Gluten-Free Granolas & Mueslis

Crisp, crunchy, satisfying homemade granola and muesli is the perfect make-ahead breakfast staple for busy weekday mornings but can be difficult to enjoy when you need to find a gluten-free version. This chapter shows you just how easy it is to create your delicious mueslis and gorgeous granolas. These home made granola and muesli recipes are very versatile and forgiving, if a particular flavouring ingredient is either not to hand or to your taste, simply substitute something else instead. This chapter does come with a health-warning, though – home-made granola/muesli is seriously addictive, you will never want to eat store-bought again!

Home made granola and muesli, once fully cooled, can be stored in any sort of air-tight container such as food storage tubs or Kilner glass jars. Alternatively, it can be bagged up into individual portions and frozen.

LEMON, BLUEBERRY & HONEY GRANOLA

GF DF V YF

Ingredients

- 10ml (2 tsp) Olive Oil
- 50ml (3 tbsp) Honey
- 3 Lemons, juiced
- 350g (4^1/$_3$ Cups) Gluten-Free Rolled Oats
- 150g (6 Cups) Organic Gluten-Free Puffed Brown Rice
- 120g (½ Cup) Lemon Curd
- 55g (²/₃ Cup) Unsweetened Desiccated Coconut
- 30g (¼ Cup) Pumpkin Seeds
- 35g (¼ Cup) Sunflower Seeds
- 120g (¾ Cup) Dried Blueberries

Directions

Preheat the oven to 140C fan, 300F, Gas Mark 4. Line two baking sheets with parchment.

In a large bowl, mix together all the dry ingredients. Mix the oil, lemon curd, honey and lemon juice in a jug and pour over the dry mix. Stir well to ensure that all the ingredients are wet. Spread onto two large baking sheets lined with baking parchment and place into the oven. Bake for a total of 45-60 mins, checking every 15mins and turning it over. The granola is ready when it is all toasted and dry.

Remove from oven and allow to cool completely. Store in a sealed container. Makes 20 servings and will keep for 3 months in a sealed airtight container. 1 portion = (40g/¹/₃ cup).

Make this Vegan? – Substitute Maple Syrup for the Honey.

Make this Oat-Free? – Omit the oats and replace with quinoa flakes.

Serves: 20   Ready In: 1hr 15 mins + cooling time

Spiced Pumpkin, Apple & Walnut Granola

GF **DF** **V** **Ve** **YF**

Ingredients

- 10ml (2 tsp) Olive Oil
- 60ml (¼ Cup) Maple Syrup
- 120ml (½ Cup) Apple Juice (Apple Cider)
- 250g (3 Cups) Gluten-Free Rolled Oats
- 120g (½ Cup) Pumpkin Purée
- 55g (²/₃ Cup) Unsweetened Desiccated Coconut
- 50g (½ Cup) Dried Apple Slices
- 1½ tsp Freshly Ground Nutmeg
- 100g (4 Cups) Organic Gluten-Free Puffed Brown Rice
- 30g (¼ Cup) Pumpkin Seeds
- 35g (¼ Cup) Sunflower Seeds
- 50g (¹/₃ Cup) Raisins
- 100g (1 Cup) Walnut Halves
- 1½ tsp Ground Ginger
- 1 tbsp Ground Cinnamon

Directions

Preheat the oven to 140C fan, 300F, Gas Mark 4. Line two baking sheets with parchment.

Chop the walnuts and dried apple slices into bite size pieces. In a large bowl, mix together all the dry ingredients. Mix the oil, maple syrup, pumpkin purée and apple juice in a jug and pour over the dry mix. Stir well to ensure that all the ingredients are damp. Spread onto two large baking sheets lined with baking parchment and place into the oven. Bake for a total of 30-45 mins, checking every 15mins and turning it over. The granola is ready when it is all toasted and dry.

Remove from oven and allow to cool completely. Store in a sealed container. Makes 20 servings and will keep for 3 months in a sealed airtight container. You can also freeze this. 1 portion = (40g/$^1/_3$ cup).

Make this Nut-Free? – Omit the walnuts, double the quantity of pumpkin and sunflower seeds and add 5g of Golden Flaxseeds.

Make this Oat-Free? – Omit the oats and replace with quinoa flakes.

Serves: 20   Ready In: 1hr 15 mins + cooling time

Banana, Maple & Pecan Nut Granola

Ingredients

- 10ml (2 tsp) Olive Oil
- 50ml (3 tbsp) Maple Syrup
- 100ml ($^1/_3$ Cup + 1 tbsp) Apple Juice (Apple Cider)
- 350g ($4^1/_3$ Cups) Gluten-Free Rolled Oats
- 150g (6 Cups) Organic Gluten-Free Puffed Brown Rice
- 55g ($^2/_3$ Cup) Unsweetened Desiccated Coconut
- 35g (¼ Cup) Pumpkin Seeds
- 30g (4 tbsp) Sunflower Seeds
- 25g (2½ tbsp) Golden Linseeds (Flaxseeds)
- 65g ($^2/_3$ Cup) Dried Banana Slices
- 65g ($^2/_3$ Cup) Pecan Nut Halves

Directions

Preheat the oven to 140C fan, 300F, Gas Mark 4. Line two baking sheets with parchment.

Chop the pecan nuts and dried banana slices into bite size pieces. In a large bowl, mix together all the dry ingredients. Mix the oil, maple syrup and apple juice in a jug and pour over the dry mix. Stir well to ensure that all the ingredients are wet. Spread onto two large baking sheets lined with baking parchment and place into the oven. Bake for a total of 45-60 mins, checking every 15mins and turning it over. The granola is ready when it is all toasted and dry.

Remove from oven and allow to cool completely. Store in a sealed container. Makes 20 servings and will keep for 3 months in a sealed airtight container. You can also freeze this. 1 portion = (40g/$^1/_3$ cup).

Make this Nut-Free? – Omit the pecans, double the quantity of pumpkin and sunflower seeds.

Make this Oat-Free? – Omit the oats and replace with quinoa flakes.

Serves: 20   Ready In: 1hr 15 mins + cooling time

Chocolate, Cherry & Hazelnut Granola GF DF V Ve YF

Ingredients

- 10ml (2 tsp) Olive Oil
- 50ml (3 tbsp) Maple Syrup
- 15g (3 tbsp) Pure Organic Gluten-Free Cocoa Powder (Dutch Process)
- 100ml ($^1/_3$ Cup + 1 tbsp) Cherry Juice
- 350g ($4^1/_3$ Cups) Gluten-Free Rolled Oats
- 150g (6 Cups) Organic Gluten-Free Puffed Brown Rice
- 55g ($^2/_3$ Cup) Unsweetened Desiccated Coconut
- 35g (¼ Cup) Pumpkin Seeds
- 30g (4 tbsp) Sunflower Seeds
- 25g (2½ tbsp) Golden Linseeds (Flaxseeds)
- 80g (½ Cup) Dried Cherries
- 65g ($^2/_3$ Cup) Cocoa Nibs
- 65g ($^2/_3$ Cup) Blanched Hazelnuts

Directions

Preheat the oven to 140C fan, 300F, Gas Mark 4. Line two baking sheets with parchment.

Roughly chop the hazelnuts and dried cherries. In a large bowl, mix together all the dry ingredients except the cocoa powder. Mix the oil, maple syrup and cherry juice in a jug, add the cocoa powder and whisk well to combine. Pour over the dry mix. Stir well to ensure that all the ingredients are wet. Spread onto two large baking sheets lined with baking parchment and place into the oven. Bake for a total of 45-60 mins, checking every 15mins and turning it over. The granola is ready when it is all toasted and dry.

Remove from oven and allow to cool completely. Stir in the chocolate chips. Store in a sealed container. Makes 20 servings and will keep for 3 months in a sealed airtight container. You can also freeze this. 1 portion = (40g/$^1/_3$ cup).

Make this Nut-Free? – Omit the hazelnuts, double the quantity of pumpkin and sunflower seeds.

Make this Oat-Free? – Omit the oats and replace with quinoa flakes.

Serves: 20   Ready In: 1hr 15 mins + cooling time

Tropical Granola

Ingredients

- 10ml (2 tsp) Olive Oil
- 30ml (2 tbsp) Maple Syrup
- 100ml ($^1/_3$ Cup + 1 tbsp) Mango or Pineapple Juice
- 350g (4$^1/_3$ Cups) Gluten-Free Rolled Oats
- 150g (6 Cups) Organic Gluten-Free Puffed Brown Rice
- 40g (½ Cup) Unsweetened Desiccated Coconut
- 35g (¼ Cup) Pumpkin Seeds
- 25g (2½ tbsp) Golden Linseeds (Flaxseeds)
- 60g (½ Cup) Dried Mango
- 60g (½ Cup) Dried Pineapple
- 40g (½ Cup) Dried Banana Slices
- 80g ($^2/_3$ Cup) Cashew Nuts

Directions

Preheat the oven to 140C fan, 300F, Gas Mark 4. Line two baking sheets with parchment.

Chop the cashew nuts and dried fruits into small pieces. In a large bowl, mix together all the dry ingredients. Mix the oil, maple syrup and juice in a jug and pour over the dry mix. Stir well to ensure that all the ingredients are wet. Spread onto two large baking sheets lined with baking parchment and place into the oven. Bake for a total of 45-60 mins, checking every 15mins and turning it over. The granola is ready when it is all toasted and dry.

Remove from oven and allow to cool completely. Store in a sealed container. Makes 20 servings and will keep for 3 months in a sealed airtight container. You can also freeze this. 1 portion = (40g/$^1/_3$ cup).

Make this Nut-Free? – Omit the pecans, double the quantity of pumpkin and sunflower seeds.

Make this Oat-Free? – Omit the oats and replace with quinoa flakes.

Serves: 20   Ready In: 1hr 15 mins + cooling time

Really Fruity & Nutty Honey Granola GF DF V YF

Ingredients

- 10ml (2 tsp) Olive Oil
- 50ml (3 tbsp) Honey
- 100ml ($^1/_3$ Cup + 1 tbsp) Orange Juice
- 35g (¼ Cup) Pumpkin Seeds
- 65g (½ Cup) Ready to Eat Apricots
- 65g (scant ½ Cup) Raisins
- 35g ($^1/_3$ Cup) Pecan Nut Halves
- 35g ($^1/_3$ Cup) Blanched Hazelnuts
- 35g (scant ½ Cup) Flaked Almonds
- 35g (4 tbsp) Brazil Nuts
- 350g ($4^1/_3$ Cups) Gluten-Free Rolled Oats
- 55g ($^2/_3$ Cup) Unsweetened Desiccated Coconut
- 150g (6 Cups) Organic Gluten-Free Puffed Brown Rice

Directions

Preheat the oven to 140C fan, 300F, Gas Mark 4. Line two baking sheets with parchment.

Chop the nuts into bite size pieces. In a large bowl, mix together all the dry ingredients. Mix the oil, honey and apple juice in a jug and pour over the dry mix. Stir well to ensure that all the ingredients are wet. Spread onto two large baking sheets lined with baking parchment and place into the oven. Bake for a total of 45-60 mins, checking every 15 mins and turning it over. The granola is ready when it is dry and toasted.

Remove from oven and allow to cool completely. Store in a sealed container. Makes 20 servings and will keep for 3 months in a sealed airtight container. 1 portion = (40g/$^1/_3$ cup).

Make this Vegan? – Substitute Maple Syrup for the Honey.

Make this Oat-Free? – Omit the oats and replace with quinoa flakes.

Serves: 20   Ready In: 1hr 15 mins + cooling time

Walnut, Apple & Cinnamon Muesli GF DF V Ve YF

Ingredients

- 350g (4¹/₃ Cups) Gluten-Free Rolled Oats
- 150g (2 Cups) Quinoa Flakes
- 35g (¼ Cup) Pumpkin Seeds
- 25g (2½ tbsp) Golden Linseeds (Flaxseeds)
- 85g (1 Cup) Dried Apple Slices
- 80g (½ Cup) Raisins
- 100g (1 Cup) Walnut Nut Halves
- 1 tbsp Ground Cinnamon

Directions

Preheat the oven to 140C fan, 300F, Gas Mark 4. Line two baking sheets with parchment.

Chop the walnut pieces and mix together with the oats, flakes and seeds. Spread over the 2 baking sheets and toast in the oven for 10 mins, turning everything over halfway through. Remove from the oven and leave to cool. Chop the dried apple slices into bite size pieces and add to the toasted mix along with the raisins and ground cinnamon. Mix well. Store in a sealed container. Makes 20 servings and will keep for 2 months in a sealed, airtight container. 1 portion = (40g/¹/₃ cup).

Make this Oat-Free? – Omit the oats and replace with quinoa flakes.

Serves: 20   **Ready In: 20 mins**

Bircher Muesli GF V Ve YF

Ingredients

- 60g (¾ cup) Gluten-Free Rolled Oats
- 150ml (²/₃ Cup) Plain Yogurt
- 15g (1 tbsp) Seedless Raisins
- 2 tsp Golden Linseeds (Flaxseeds)
- ¼ tsp Ground Cinnamon
- 1 Medium Apple
- ¼ Lemon
- 8 blanched Hazelnuts
- 2 tsp Maple Syrup

Directions

Roughly chop the hazelnuts. In a sealable container, mix together with the rolled oats, seeds, raisins, yogurt and maple syrup. Seal and leave in the fridge overnight. The following morning, grate the apple (skin on) and squeeze over the juice from the lemon quarter. Fold into the oat mixture, divide into two bowls and serve.

Serves: 2   **Ready In: 5 mins** (plus soaking overnight)

Red & Blue Berry Burst Muesli

GF **DF** **V** **Ve** **YF**

Ingredients

- 350g (4⅓ Cups) Gluten-Free Rolled Oats
- 150g (2 Cups) Quinoa Flakes
- 35g (¼ Cup) Pumpkin Seeds
- 30g (4 tbsp) Sunflower Seeds
- 25g (2 ½ tbsp) Golden Linseeds (Flaxseeds)
- 65g (½ Cup) Dried Cranberries
- 65g (½ Cup) Dried Blueberries
- 35g (¼ Cup) Dried Apples
- 60g (¾ Cup) Desiccated Coconut (unsweetened)
- 35g (¼ Cup) Blanched Hazelnuts
- 35g (½ Cup) Flaked Almonds
- 35g (⅓ Cup) Walnuts

Directions

Preheat the oven to 140C fan, 300F, Gas Mark 4. Line two baking sheets with parchment.

Roughly chop the walnuts and hazelnut and mix together with the oats, flakes, seeds and coconut. Spread over the 2 baking sheets and toast in the oven for 10 minutes, turning everything over halfway through. Remove from the oven and leave to cool.

Roughly chop the dried apples. Combine together with the flaked almonds, cranberries, blueberries and cooled toasted mix. Store in a sealed container. Makes 20 servings and will keep for 2 months in a sealed, airtight container. 1 portion = = (40g/⅓ cup).

Make this Oat-Free? – Omit the oats and replace with quinoa flakes.

Serves: 20   Ready In: 20 mins

Breakfast Eggs

Buying the best quality and freshest ingredients that you can afford is always important for any keen cook and foodie and this is especially true when it comes to eggs. I always use free range, organic eggs. Luckily, I am able to buy mine from the lovely 'Chicken Lady' across the road so they are as fresh as can be and from very happy chickens who are free to roam and forage. These gorgeous eggs (pictured above) come in a variety of sizes and beautiful shell colours (for their special close-up, I've also cleaned mine so that they are free of the organic matter that they also come with)! Where ever you source your eggs from, make sure that they are as fresh as can be when cooking with them to obtain the best and tastiest results from your endeavours.

Poached Eggs with Watercress Sauce

GF NF OF YF

Ingredients

- 2 Slices Gluten-Free Bread
- 2 UK Medium (US Large) Free Range Egg
- 100g (3 Cups) Watercress
- 75ml (5 tbsp) Crème Fraîche
- 5g (2 tsp) freshly grated Parmesan Cheese
- Pinch freshly grated Nutmeg
- Pinch freshly ground Black Pepper
- Pinch Sea (Kosher) Salt

Directions

Warm the crème fraîche in a small saucepan over a low heat. Remove the watercress leaves from the stalks and discard the stalks. Add the watercress leaves to the saucepan and cook until the watercress has wilted (about 3 mins). Season with a pinch of freshly grated nutmeg and ground black pepper and stir in the grated parmesan cheese. Then taking care with hot liquids, transfer to a liquidiser or food processor and whizz in until smooth. Return to the saucepan and keep warm over a low heat.

Meanwhile, bring another saucepan filled with water to barely simmering point. Once the watercress sauce is ready, crack each egg into the water and cook to your liking (3 mins for a soft poached egg, 5 mins for a firm poach). Whilst the eggs are poaching, toast the bread. Once the eggs are cooked, remove from the water with a slotted spoon and drain on kitchen towel. To serve, place a slice of toast on a warm plate, top with a poached egg and spoon over half the watercress sauce.

Make this Dairy-Free? – Simply use a dairy-free alternative cream instead of the crème fraîche and add a squeeze of lemon juice to the watercress sauce.

Serves: 2   Ready In: 25 mins

Coddled Eggs with Roasted Asparagus & Parma Ham "Soldiers"

Ingredients

- 8 fresh, large Asparagus Spears
- 4 slices Parma Ham
- 2 UK Large (US Extra Large) Free Range Eggs
- 2 tbsp Crème Fraîche
- 1 tsp Olive Oil
- Pinch Sea (Kosher) Salt
- Pinch Freshly Ground Black Pepper
- Pinch Freshly Grated Nutmeg

Note: Egg coddling cups are very pretty, heat-safe ceramic cups with screw-on lids that can be purchased from specialist kitchen equipment stores. However, if you don't have any coddlers (or the inclination to buy some), then you can use heat-proof ramekins and kitchen film instead. The main thing that needs to be achieved is to keep the eggs separate from the water and steam that cooks them.

Directions

Preheat the oven to 180C fan, 350F, Gas Mark 6.

Grease two egg coddlers (or ramekins) and a baking tray with the olive oil.

Trim the woody ends off the asparagus spears. Cut the slices of Parma ham in half and then wrap each asparagus spear with ½ a slice of ham. Place onto the greased baking sheet and season with freshly ground black pepper.

Spoon ½ tbsp of crème fraîche into the bottom of each ramekin, then crack in a fresh egg and top with ½ tbsp of crème fraîche. Season with a pinch of sea (kosher) salt and a light grating of nutmeg.

Lay a triple thickness of kitchen paper towel into the bottom of a saucepan, then fill with enough boiling water to come just below the rim of the coddlers/ramekins. Place the saucepan over medium heat and bring the water back to simmering point.

If using proper coddlers, screw their lids on tightly. Alternatively, fully seal the ramekins with a double layer of kitchen film. Carefully lower the sealed eggs into the simmering water, cover with the pan lid then simmer on low for 10 mins (or 2-3 mins longer if you prefer your eggs yolks completely cooked through).

Meanwhile, place the asparagus tips into the oven to roast.

Protecting your hands from the heat, carefully remove the coddlers/ramekins from the saucepan, unscrew lids/remove kitchen film, and serve immediately with roasted asparagus "soldiers" on the side.

Make this Dairy-Free? – Simply use a dairy-free alternative cream instead of the crème fraîche mixed with a squeeze of lemon juice.

Make this Vegetarian? – Omit the Parma ham and toss the asparagus spears in a tsp of olive oil before roasting.

Serves: 2   Ready In: 15 mins

Spinach Omelette

Ingredients

- 2 UK Large (US Extra Large) Free Range Eggs
- 15g (1 tbsp) Soft Cheese
- 90g (3 Cups) Baby Spinach
- ½ tsp Olive Oil
- Pinch Freshly Ground Black Pepper
- Pinch Freshly Ground Nutmeg

Directions

In a bowl, lightly whisk the eggs until frothy and season with freshly ground black pepper. Warm the olive oil in a sauté pan over a medium heat. Reduce heat to low and add eggs. Cook the eggs gently, using a spatula to bring the set mixture from around the edges of the pan into the centre.

Meanwhile, put the spinach in a heatproof bowl, and microwave for 1½ mins. Stir through the soft cheese and add a pinch of freshly ground nutmeg. When the omelette is almost completely set, spread the spinach mixture onto ½ of the omelette, and fold the other half over the top. Slide onto a warm plate and serve.

Make this Dairy-Free? – Simply use a dairy-free soft white cheese instead of the soft cheese.

Serves: 1   Ready In: 10 mins

Herby Cherry Tomato Omelette GF NF OF V YF

Ingredients

- 2 UK Large (US Extra Large) Free Range Eggs
- 7 Cherry Tomatoes
- ½ tsp Dried Marjoram or 1 tsp Fresh Marjoram, finely chopped
- 1 Small Shallot
- 1 tsp Olive Oil, divided
- 3½ tbsp (25g) Cheddar Cheese, grated
- Pinch Kosher/Sea Salt
- Pinch Ground Black Pepper

Directions

Start by thinly slicing the shallot and cutting the cherry tomatoes in half. Heat ½ tsp olive oil in a non-stick sauté pan over a medium high. Add the sliced shallot and cook for 2-3 mins until starting to brown and soften. Then add the halved tomatoes, cut side down. Continue to cook for 5 mins, then turn the tomatoes over and cook for a further 3 mins. Remove the mixture to a small bowl and season with the marjoram and a pinch of salt and pepper.

Wipe out the sauté pan, add the remaining ½ tsp olive oil and return to a medium heat. In a bowl, lightly whisk the eggs until frothy. Season with freshly ground black pepper. Add the egg mixture to the pan, tipping the pan so that it covers the base. Draw the cooked edges into the centre of the pan, then tip the pan to allow the still liquid egg to reach the sides. As soon as the omelette is set, return the herbed tomatoes to one half of the omelette, then scatter over the grated cheese and flip over the other half of the omelette. Slide out of the pan, onto a warm plate and serve.

Make this Dairy-Free? – Simply use a dairy-free alternative cheese instead of the cheddar cheese.

Serves: 1   Ready In: 20 mins

Cheesy Baked Eggs Florentine

Ingredients

- 250g (8 Cups) Raw Spinach
- 100ml (½ Cup) Fresh Milk
- ½ tbsp Cornflour/Corn starch
- ½ tsp Swiss Vegetable Bouillon Powder
- ½ tsp Gluten-Free Dry Mustard Powder
- 2 tbsp (14g) grated Cheddar Cheese
- 1 tbsp finely grated Parmesan Cheese
- 2 UK Large (US Extra Large) Free Range Eggs
- Pinch Ground Black Pepper
- Pinch Sea (Kosher) Salt
- Pinch Freshly Ground Nutmeg

Directions

Preheat the oven to 180C fan, 375F, Gas Mark 6.

Rinse the spinach in a colander and shake off excess moistures. Heat a non-stick saucepan over a medium heat and add the spinach. Season with freshly ground black pepper and a pinch of sea (kosher) salt. Cook until wilted. Use a slotted spoon and divide evenly between two oven-proof ramekins, creating a well in the centre of each portion.

Rinse the pan out. Mix the cornflour (corn starch) with a little of the milk to a smooth paste. Heat the remaining milk in the saucepan over a medium heat. Stir in the cornflour (corn starch) paste; continue stirring until the sauce thickens. Add the stock powder, mustard powder and nutmeg, mix well then stir in the grated Parmesancheese and mix again.

Crack one egg into each of the wells in the spinach. Spoon over the cheese sauce and sprinkle with the grated cheddar cheese. Bake in a preheated oven for 10-14 minutes (depending on how well cooked you prefer your eggs). Serve hot.

Make this Dairy-Free? – Simply use a dairy-free cheese instead of the Parmesan and Cheddar and use a dairy-free milk alternative.

Serves: 2   Ready In: 20 mins

EASY EGGS BENEDICT GF NF OF

Ingredients

- 2 Slices thickly sliced Ham
- 180g (6 Cups) Baby Spinach
- 45ml (3 tbsp) Crème Fraîche
- Pinch Dried Tarragon
- 2 Gluten-Free Crumpets
- 2 UK Large (US Extra Large) Free Range Eggs
- 1 tsp White Wine Vinegar
- 10g (2 tsp) Sunflower Spread
- Pinch Freshly Ground Nutmeg
- ¼ tsp Freshly Ground Black Pepper
- Pinch Sea (Kosher) Salt

Directions

Start by making the tarragon sauce. In a small saucepan over a low heat, warm the crème fraîche, vinegar, dried tarragon and black pepper. Whisk well to combine, if it is too thick, slacken with a splash of hot water.

Bring a large pan of water to the boil. Break the eggs into 2 separate tea cups. Put the gluten-free crumpets onto toast. Briskly swirl the boiling water to form a vortex and slide in the eggs. Cook for 3-4 mins (or longer, depending on your preference), then remove with a slotted spoon and drain onto a piece of kitchen towel.

Meanwhile, put the spinach in a heatproof bowl, and microwave for 1½ mins until wilted. Season with a pinch of sea (kosher) salt, freshly ground black pepper and nutmeg.

Spread the toasted crumpets with the sunflower spread and place onto warm serving plates. Top each crumpet with half of the spinach, followed by a slice of ham then a poached egg and then drizzle the sauce over the top. Sprinkle with a twist of freshly ground black pepper and serve.

Make this Dairy-Free? – Simply use a dairy-free alternative cream instead of the crème fraîche and add a squeeze of lemon juice to the tarragon sauce.

Make this Vegetarian? – Replace the ham with 2 rashers of cooked Quorn Bacon.

Serves: 2   Ready In: 15 mins

Mexican Breakfast Scramble GF NF OF V YF

Ingredients

- ½ Red Bell Pepper, deseeded
- 60g (½ Cup) Mushrooms
- 80g (½ Cup) canned Black Beans
- 2 tbsp fresh Coriander (Cilantro)
- 4 UK Medium (US Large) Free Range Eggs
- 20g (2 tbsp) Mature Cheese, grated

- 125g (4 Cups) Baby Spinach
- Pinch Ground Black Pepper
- 2 Large Tomatoes
- ½ Lime, Juiced
- ¼ tsp ground Cumin
- 2 shakes Tabasco Sauce

- 1 Red Onion
- Pinch Sea (Kosher) Salt
- ½ tsp Oregano
- 1 tsp Butter
- 1 tsp Olive Oil
- ½ tsp Chilli Flakes

Directions

Preferably, make the Salsa the night before to allow the flavours to develop fully. Place the tomatoes in a heat-proof bowl and covering with boiling water. Wait for 1 min, then carefully remove from the bowl with a slotted spoon. When they are cool enough to handle, slip the skins off. Set 1 tomato aside for later.

Finely dice half of the red onion and 1 tomato. Mix together the rinsed, drained black beans, diced onion and tomato with the juice of half a lime, the minced fresh coriander (cilantro), ground cumin, chilli flakes and oregano. Season with a pinch of black pepper and set aside to allow the salsa flavours to develop (preferably overnight).

In the morning, preheat the oven on low 80C fan, 175F, Gas Mark ¼. Put an oven-proof serving plate into warm. Next, thinly slice the remaining half of the red onion along with the red pepper and mushrooms. Warm the olive oil in a heavy-bottom non-stick sauté pan over a medium heat. Sauté the sliced vegetables, until they are softened and slightly golden, about 5 mins. Cut the remaining tomato in half. Scoop out the seeds and discard. Dice the tomato. Add the baby spinach and diced tomato, then cook through until the spinach is wilted, about 3 mins. Transfer the vegetables onto the warm plate, cover with kitchen foil and put into the oven to stay warm. Have the salsa and grated cheese ready to go.

In a bowl, lightly whisk together the eggs until frothy. Return the sauté pan to a medium heat and add the tsp of butter. Reduce heat to low and add eggs, scrambling until cooked through, about 3 minutes and immediately remove from the heat. Divide the scrambled eggs between two warm dinner plates, spoon over the salsa and grated cheese. Season to taste with Tabasco Sauce.

Serves: 2   Ready In: 45 mins

Red Pepper & Cottage Cheese Frittatas

Ingredients

- ½ Red Bell Pepper, diced
- 2 Large (Extra Large) Free Range Eggs
- 4 tbsp Cottage Cheese
- 1 tbsp freshly grated Parmesan Cheese
- 2 Spring Onions (Scallions), sliced
- 2 tsp Freshly Chopped Parsley
- Pinch Freshly Grated Nutmeg
- Pinch Freshly Ground Black Pepper
- Pinch Sea (Kosher) Salt

Directions

Preheat the oven to 180C fan, 350F, Gas Mark 6. Grease 2 oven-proof ramekins and place on a baking sheet.

Remove the seeds and pith from the red pepper and dice. Finely slice the spring onions (scallions). Chop the parsley.

Break in the eggs into a bowl. Season with sea (kosher) salt, pepper and a generous grating of nutmeg and lightly whisk. Fold in the cottage cheese, red pepper, spring onions (scallions) and chopped parsley. Divide the mixture between the ramekins and sprinkle over the grated parmesan cheese. Bake for 18-20 mins or until just set. Leave to cool a little before removing from the tin and serving.

These can be eaten warm or cooled and packed into a sealed container for breakfast on the go.

Serves: 2   Ready In: 15 mins

Resources – Gluten-Free Ingredients

Health Food & Online Stores with a wide range of Gluten-Free Ingredients
US – TraderJoes.com, WholeFoodsMarket.com, Amazon.com
UK – HollandAndBarrett.com, Amazon.co.uk

Gluten-Free Flours & Other Baking Ingredients
US - Wellbees.com, Honeyville.com, BobsRedMill.com/
UK – DovesFarm.co.uk, Shipton-Mill.com,

Gluten-Free Sausages and other Meat Products
US – Applegate.com
UK – TheBlackFarmer.com

Gluten-Free Bread, Wraps & Baked Goods
US - UdisGlutenFree.com
UK - NewburnBakehouse.com

A NOTE FROM THE AUTHOR

Your Feedback

Thank you for choosing my Cookbook. I would love to know what you think of the recipes in this book, are any particular favourites? I would be most grateful you were able to leave a book review on the website that you purchased it from.

Further Gluten-Free Books & Bonus Free Giveaway

If you have enjoyed the recipes in this cookbook, you may also be interested in further books in this series:

Gluten Free Wheat Free
Easy Baking, Bread & Meals
Getting Started Recipes Cookbook.

Your Bonus FREE Giveaway

As a special Thank You to my readers, I have available an exclusive & free special bonus. Sign up for my Readers Group Newsletter and receive a FREE copy of the *Gluten Free & Wheat Free Vegetarian Snacks Recipe Booklet.*

To receive your free PDF copy of this booklet, you just need to visit http://goo.gl/Km3H1K and let me know where to email it to.

Let's Stay Connected

Please do also take a look at my author blog, MillyWhiteCooks.com.

As well as details on my full range of cookbooks, you will also find articles and helpful information on:

- Ingredients
- Cooking Techniques
- Equipment
- Health News
- Nutrition Information
- Special Offers

Every month I share a new menu of the month, showcasing recipes from my collection. You can find me on social media too:

 MillyWhiteCooks.com   facebook.com/MillyWhiteCooks

 pinterest.com/MillyWhiteCooks   instagram.com/MillyWhiteCooks

 twitter.com/MillyWhiteCooks   plus.google.com/+MillywhitecooksBooks/posts

INDEX

Printed in Great Britain
by Amazon

33194421R00041